MATERIALS

Written by
Martin Hollins

Illustrated by
Julian Baker, Jan Hill and John Shipperbottom

Edited by
Caroline White

Designed by
Charlotte Crace

Picture research by
Helen Taylor

CONTENTS

Using materials

Throughout the world, people need food and drink, homes and clothes, and ways of travelling and communicating with one another. Materials are used for all these things.

There are thousands of different types of materials. Some come from nature, such as rocks, clay, wood, wool and silk. Other materials are made (manufactured) by people. Metals and plastics are manufactured from natural substances called raw materials.

This book is all about the natural and manufactured materials that we use. Some materials were discovered by ancient craft workers. They learnt to shape stones, make pots and bricks from clay, weave cloth and get metals from rocks in the ground. In more recent times, scientists have invented new materials. These are used to design new products to make our lives more comfortable and interesting.

3

Natural materials

① wood
② stone
③ oil
④ wool
⑤ silk
⑥ cotton
⑦ leather
⑧ gold
⑨ gemstones

Manufactured materials

⑩ rubber
⑪ steel
⑫ nylon
⑬ PVC
⑭ aluminium
⑮ paint
⑯ glass
⑰ pottery
⑱ paper
⑲ brick
⑳ plastic

Choosing materials

Imagine a bike made out of rubber or a bed made out of concrete. Not very useful, are they? Rubber and concrete do not behave in the way that is needed for bikes to work and beds to be comfortable. Their properties are not suitable. When we make or build something, materials with the right properties have to be chosen.

Building a mountain bike

The frame of a mountain bike has to stand up to the cyclist's weight and the shock forces when riding on bumpy ground. Steel tubes are used because they are strong and rigid. The tubes are hollow to keep the bike as light as possible, so it is not too tiring to ride.

The chain and brake cables carry the forces which drive and stop the bike. Steel links and wires are used to make them strong and flexible.

The chain and cogs have to be very smooth to move easily. Oil is used to lubricate them.

The wheels are made of aluminium. This is a very light metal.

Tyres give a smoother ride. They are made of rubber filled with air. Rubber is an elastic material and will return to its normal shape after being squashed or stretched.

The saddle is made of polythene. Polythene is a plastic material and is easily moulded into a comfortable seat.

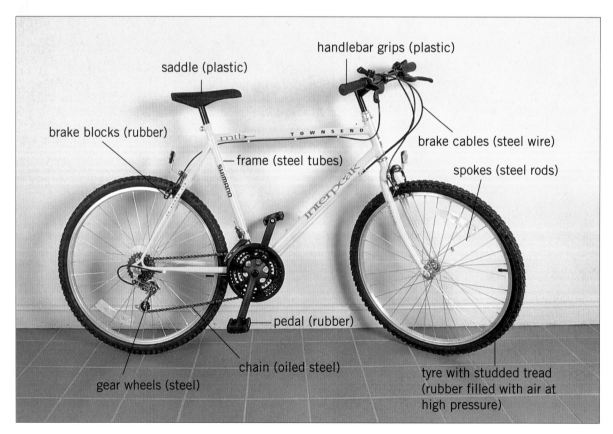

saddle (plastic)

handlebar grips (plastic)

brake blocks (rubber)

frame (steel tubes)

brake cables (steel wire)

spokes (steel rods)

pedal (rubber)

chain (oiled steel)

gear wheels (steel)

tyre with studded tread (rubber filled with air at high pressure)

Materials used to build a mountain bike

A car is tested for strength on a four-poster rig.

Handlebar grips are moulded out of plastic or rubber. Plastic is an insulator, whereas metal is a conductor. Covering the metal handlebars with plastic makes them feel warmer to touch.

Brake blocks need to be rough so that friction between them and the wheel stops the bike. They are made of tough rubber.

Cycle helmets are made of strong plastic lined with soft foam plastic. The foam plastic makes the helmet comfortable to wear and absorbs some of the impact force in the case of an accident.

Testing materials

Materials are tested scientifically to see if they have the right properties for the job. They are stretched, squashed, rubbed and bashed in laboratories. Bikes are tested on mountains and special rigs.

Solids, liquids and gases

All substances can be grouped into solids, liquids or gases. Solids have a shape and a volume. Liquids have a volume but no shape. They are runny and can be poured into a container. Gases have no volume or shape and will spread everywhere.

Properties of water

Like most liquids, water is runny and mixes easily with other substances. When sugar is dissolved in water, the sugar particles mix with the water particles. This makes a mixture which has the runny property of water and the sweetness of sugar.

Water can easily be turned into a solid. If it is cooled to a temperature of 0 °C, it becomes ice. The water particles in ice are held together strongly, like people holding hands. As a liquid, the particles are held together weakly, like people holding threads. If water is heated to a temperature of 100 °C, it turns to the gas known as steam. Here the same water particles can move freely because they are not joined at all.

When steam hits a cold surface, it will condense and turn back to water. Similarly, ice melts back to water when it is heated.

steam

W

ice

A geyser sends up hot steam created when water is heated deep underground.

How materials change

There are 92 different chemical elements from which everything on Earth is made. Each element is made of tiny particles called atoms. These are too small to see even with a microscope.

Water is made from two elements, oxygen and hydrogen. The oxygen atoms join with the hydrogen atoms to form larger particles called molecules.

Materials can change when their particles are heated or mixed with other particles. If iron becomes damp, the iron atoms join with oxygen atoms to make a new substance called rust. In the kitchen, toast burns and turns bread into the element carbon. When a new substance is produced, the change is called a chemical reaction. Chemical reactions are going on all around us, as we cook a meal or drive a car. Dissolving sugar in water is not a chemical reaction, because the sugar can be separated from the water by leaving the solution to dry.

The iron in an opened tin can turns to rust if it becomes damp.

Bread turns into carbon if it is burnt.

Materials science

Scientists study the properties of materials. This helps them to invent new materials. Carbon is a very common element found as soot (from fires), charcoal (on burnt toast) and diamond (in rocks). Carbon has recently been turned into several new materials. Turn to the end of the book to find out more.

Rocks

The Earth is made of rocky materials. The ground beneath our feet is called the Earth's crust. It is made of hard rock covered in soil or water. Deep under the Earth's crust lies a layer of red-hot liquid rock, called magma.

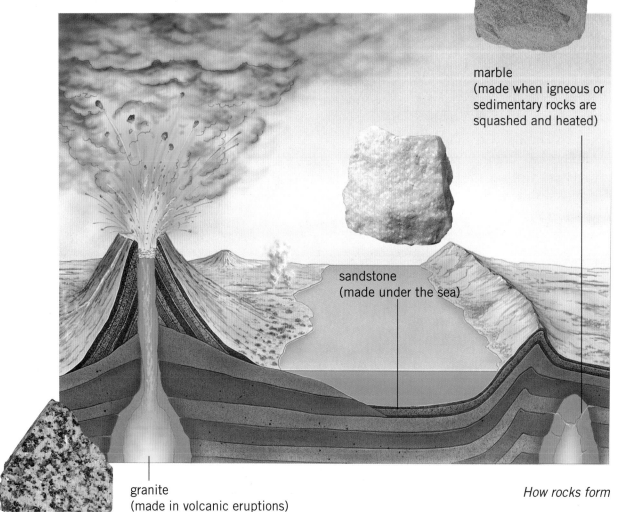

marble
(made when igneous or
sedimentary rocks are
squashed and heated)

sandstone
(made under the sea)

granite
(made in volcanic eruptions)

How rocks form

There are three main types of rock: igneous, sedimentary and metamorphic.

Igneous rocks form when volcanoes erupt. Hot liquid rock from inside the Earth bursts through the surface and then cools and hardens on the crust.

The action of the weather and sea breaks pieces of igneous rock into small particles. The particles are washed into the sea as sediments. After a long time, the pressure of the sea compresses the layers of sediment to form **sedimentary** rocks.

When igneous or sedimentary rocks are pushed back into the Earth, they are changed by great heat and pressure underground to form **metamorphic** rocks.

Stone for building

Rock has been used throughout history to build homes. It is usually cut or broken into convenient shapes called stones. Igneous and metamorphic rocks are hard and strong. They do not weather easily. Sedimentary rocks are softer and easier to cut. They are quite strong, but can be eroded by acid rain. Cutting rock is hard work and makes stone an expensive building material.

Name of rock	Type of rock	Use
① granite	igneous	kerbstones (stands up to hard wear and tear)
② sandstone	sedimentary	church (easy to carve into statues)
③ limestone	sedimentary	monument (easy to cut and hard-wearing)
④ marble	metamorphic	bank steps (hard-wearing and impressive)
⑤ slate	metamorphic	cottage roof (strong and can be split into thin sheets)

Stone is often used today only for special features such as fireplaces. Concrete and brick are much cheaper materials to use. Look at the table above to find out what types of rock have been used to build the village in the picture below.

Stone used for building

Minerals

The Earth's rocky crust is made up of chemicals called minerals. These are used to make other materials, such as metals. Minerals can also form crystals inside rocks. Some crystals are so attractive they are cut, polished and made into jewellery.

The same chemical can exist in many different forms. Let's look at an example using the chemical aluminium oxide.

Aluminium oxide is made of aluminium and oxygen. It is a very common chemical in the Earth, often found in weathered rocks as the mineral bauxite. Bauxite is used to make the metal aluminium.

When aluminium oxide cools from hot liquid rock, it forms crystals of the mineral corundum. Rubies (red) and sapphires (blue) are both corundum. They get their colour from small amounts of other chemicals in the aluminium oxide.

Pure aluminium oxide is called alumina. This white powder is used in household cleaning materials.

Minerals and their uses

Magnetite (iron and oxygen) is used to make iron.

Pyrite (iron and sulphur) is also used to make iron. Its other name is 'fool's gold', because of its appearance.

Malachite (copper, carbon and oxygen) is used to make copper and green paint. It is also used as a gemstone.

Quartz (silicon and oxygen) can have many coloured forms, including the gemstones amethyst (purple), rose quartz (pink) and onyx (coloured layers, which are often brown).

Talc is a smooth, soft mineral used to make talcum powder. It is also used to make paint, soap and paper.

ruby

cut sapphire

alumina

bauxite

Different forms of aluminium oxide

magnetite

pyrite

talc

quartz

malachite

Some common minerals

Gemstones and jewels

Minerals are used in jewellery as natural or cut crystals and as polished gemstones. Some gemstones are very valuable because they are so rare and beautiful.

Diamond is perhaps the most famous gemstone. As well as being quite rare, it has two special properties. First, it is the hardest natural substance; and secondly, it bends light to produce brilliant rainbow sparkles. The sparkles are most effective when each diamond is cut and polished in the best way possible for that particular stone. The Koh-i-noor (meaning 'mountain of light') is a famous diamond from India. It now sits in the Queen Mother's crown.

Did you know?
Diamond is so hard that it can only be cut with another diamond.

The Koh-i-noor is one of the world's largest cut diamonds.

Clay and brick

The Earth's rocky crust is broken down by the action of the sea, weather and living things to produce small particles of rock: soil, sand and clay. These particles stick together when wet to form materials that are easy to mould into different shapes. They can also be turned into strong building materials by heating or mixing them with chemicals.

Clay

Clay is made up of the tiniest particles of rock. Clay sticks together well when moist, and hardens as it dries. Homes have been built of clay for thousands of years because it is much easier to use than rocks or stone.

Jericho (in Jordan) is one of the world's oldest cities. Remaining parts of the city walls show they were built from lumps of clay over seven thousand years ago.

The walls of Jericho were built using clay bricks in the shape of short French loaves.

Jericho is in the desert. Clay is still a popular building material in many hot dry countries. In Mexico and the southern states of the USA, adobe houses are made from clay. The clay absorbs heat from the hot desert sun during the day, and then releases it at night when the temperature drops.

Clay is not a very strong material and turns to mud in wet weather. Before brick became widely used in Britain, clay walls were built around woven wooden 'wattles' to give them extra strength. The walls were then painted to make them waterproof. This type of wall is known as 'wattle and daub'.

Adobe houses are cool during the day and warm at night.

Rebuilding a fifteenth-century cottage made of wattle and daub

Brick

Bricks are made by heating clay to a high temperature in a kiln. The particles stick together to form a strong material.

Bricks were first used over five thousand years ago in Mesopotamia (now Iraq) and were later used by the Romans. Houses in Britain were made of wood until the Great Fire of London destroyed much of the wooden city in 1666. Most homes in Britain today are built of brick.

There are many types of brick. Special processes can make them stronger, heat-resistant or waterproof. Bricks used for building houses are not waterproof. Houses need a 'damp-proof' course to stop water soaking up from the ground.

Walls are built using different patterns of brick. The patterns are called 'bonds'. Some bonds are stronger than others, but most are simply for decoration. Look around your neighbourhood to see how many different bonds you can find.

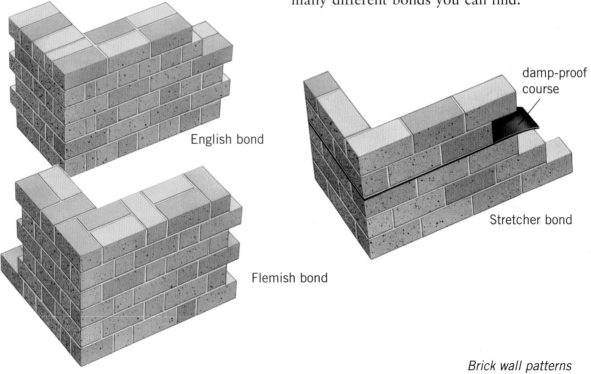

English bond

Flemish bond

damp-proof course

Stretcher bond

Brick wall patterns

Cement and concrete

Cement and concrete are manufactured from rocks and earth. They are important building materials because they have greater strength than clay or bricks.

Cement is manufactured at a cement factory.

Cement and mortar

Cement is made by mixing dry clay with crushed limestone rock. The mixture is heated to a high temperature so that a chemical reaction takes place.

The Romans made a kind of cement two thousand years ago. In 1824, Joseph Aspdin invented the cement used today.

He called it Portland cement, because when hard it resembles a type of limestone used for building called Portland stone.

Mortar is the 'glue' used to stick bricks or concrete blocks together. It is made by mixing cement with sand and water.

Concrete

Concrete is made by mixing cement with sand, stones and water. The cement hardens to hold all the stony particles together. As no heat is needed, concrete is cheaper and easier to make than bricks.

Concrete is a strong material and needs no protection from the weather. Lorries carry loads of ready-mixed concrete to building sites. Here it is used to make roads and foundations of buildings.

A mixer lorry delivers concrete from the factory to the building site.

Large buildings such as office blocks and tower blocks are usually built of reinforced concrete. This a strong combination of concrete and steel. The concrete is like stone and is very hard to crush. The steel inside is tough and does not bend or stretch.

Concrete can be strengthened by pouring it over steel rods.

Ceramics

Pottery and glass are ceramics. This group of materials is made by heating clay or sand with chemicals. The rocky particles stick together and then cool to form hard, brittle materials.

Pottery

Pottery is made from clay. Clay is easy to shape or mould when moist, and becomes hard and brittle as it dries. Clay objects must be heated, or 'fired', in a special oven called a kiln to make them strong.

Different clays produce different types of pottery. Earthenware pots are made from a cheap clay. The clay is fired at around 1000 °C to create a rough surface through which water can pass. Flowerpots are manufactured in this way.

Some clays are fired at even higher temperatures to make waterproof pottery called stoneware. Drainpipes are made of stoneware pottery.

Porcelain is made from a fine white clay called kaolin. This type of pottery is often called 'china', because the process for making it was invented in China in AD 700. Porcelain is used to make delicate cups, saucers and plates. It also has many uses in industry, because it is a good electrical insulator and does not react with other chemicals.

pylon insulator made from porcelain

stoneware drainpipe

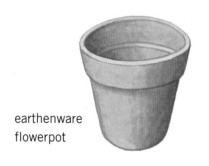

earthenware flowerpot

porcelain cup

Different types of pottery

Shaping pots

Clay can be moulded in many different ways. You may have made a coil pot or a slab pot at school. The quickest way to make round pots by hand is to use a potter's wheel. This needs a lot of practice, as you will find out if you try! In pottery factories, pots are spun and shaped automatically by machines.

Teapots being made on a potter's wheel

Glaze

Earthenware pots can be made waterproof by coating the fired pot with a glaze. The glaze is made by mixing sand with other chemicals. The mixture is heated to a high temperature until it melts. As the mixture cools, it forms a glassy surface to the pot.

Glazes can be different colours depending on the chemicals used.

Glass

Glass was invented in the Middle East over four thousand years ago. It is made by heating together sand and other chemicals. The mixture hardens as it cools, but never turns into a solid. In some ways, glass is like a very sticky liquid.

Did you know?
Old windows are thicker at the bottom than the top, because the glass slowly runs down over the years.

Molten glass can be formed into many different shapes. The Ancient Egyptians discovered how to shape it round a core to make bottles about five thousand years ago. In 100 BC, the blowpipe was invented. It is still used today for blowing glass into beautiful shapes.

Molten glass on the end of a metal tube can be blown into many different shapes.

Newly made glass bottles on a factory's conveyor belt

A ribbon of float glass slowly cools on rollers at the factory.

Float glass

Glass is used to make windows because of its transparent property. To see through glass clearly, it must have a very smooth surface. British scientist Alastair Pilkington invented a new process to produce large sheets of smooth glass in 1956. The glass was called float glass and soon became the standard glass for windows.

Float glass is made by floating molten glass on a bath of molten tin. The glass naturally forms a layer 6 millimetres thick, just right for windows. It is carefully cooled until solid enough to be rolled up. Look at the reflection in the photograph above to see how smooth the surface becomes. When the glass needs unrolling, heat is gently applied.

Safety glass

Glass is hard but brittle and can break into very sharp pieces. The glass in car windscreens is made by bonding together thin layers. This stops it from splintering in road accidents.

Lenses and mirrors

Glass can be ground and polished to make lenses for use in spectacles, telescopes, cameras and microscopes. Lenses bend light to make things appear clearer or larger. Mirrors reflect light and are made from coated glass.

Natural fibres

Natural fibres come from plants and animals. Cotton is one of the most widely used plant fibres. Wool and silk are important animal fibres. On their own, fibres are not very strong. They are spun together into thread or yarn and then woven into fabric.

Fibres from animals

Most people find they need a 'second skin' to keep their bodies warm. The first clothes were made from hairy animal skins thousands of years ago. Even today some people wear coats made of fur. Leather is made from animal skins that have been shaved of the hairs. The clever step was to use the hairs without killing the animal.

Sheep shearing

Mammals have hair to insulate them from the cold. Sheep are protected by their wool during the winter months. In spring, when they no longer need their coats, the farmer cuts off the wool. Because the hairs are curly, they hold together while the sheep is being sheared.

Sheep and goats have been bred for their wool for thousands of years. Different types of sheep produce different types of wool. Merino sheep from Australia and New Zealand have long fine wool, while cashmere and mohair are very soft wools which come from Himalayan goats. Herdwick sheep from the north of Britain produce various shades of brown wool.

Spider's webs are made of fibres. So far no one has found a way to make clothes from them. A caterpillar called the silkworm makes a fibre in a similar way. It squirts a liquid through a fine tube in its body called a spinneret. When the thread has hardened, the silkworm spins a cocoon to protect itself as it changes into a butterfly. The silk fibre is often over a kilometre long. It can be unwound by humans and re-spun for making silk clothes.

Silkworm spinning a silk cocoon

Fibres from plants

Many plants have strong fibres in their
stems and leaves made from a substance
called cellulose. These fibres are used to
make all kinds of materials. Raffia is
made from dried palm leaves. It is used as
garden string or woven into mats and
bags. Tough stem fibres of jute and hemp
are made into sacks and rope. Fibres from
flax plants are woven together to make
the strong, smooth cloth called linen.

*Palm leaves are used
to make raffia.*

Picking cotton bolls in Egypt

Cotton fibres are soft and hard-wearing.
They are attached to the seeds inside
cotton bolls. After the bolls have been
picked, the fibres are separated in a
machine called a gin. The cotton fibres
are then spun into threads.

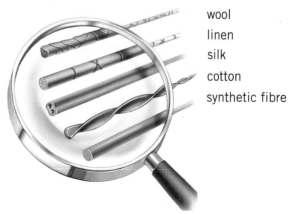

wool
linen
silk
cotton
synthetic fibre

Looking at fibres under a magnifying glass

Wood

Wood comes from the trunk and branches of trees. Its fibre structure gives wood many useful properties. Wood is strong and flexible, can easily be cut and shaped, and is usually light enough to float.

The trunk and branches are made up of four layers. The heartwood is in the very centre and gives the tree its strength. The sapwood has tiny tubes which carry water and nutrients up from the ground. These tubes give wood its fibre structure. A new layer of wood grows under the bark each year, making the tree wider and wider.

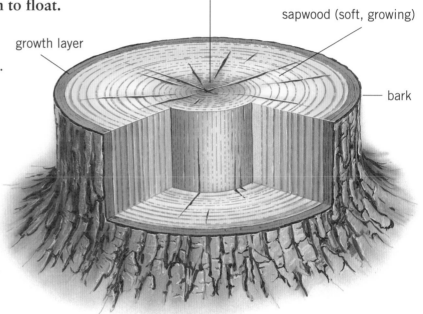

heartwood (hard, old)

sapwood (soft, growing)

growth layer

bark

The structure of wood

A cross-section of pine has been magnified to show the fibre structure of wood.

There are two main types of wood: hardwoods and softwoods.

Hardwood trees, such as beech and oak, grow slowly and have broad leaves. Hardwoods are strong and hard, and they rot very slowly. This makes them useful for building.

Softwood trees, such as pine and spruce, grow quickly and have needle-shaped leaves. Softwoods are often cheaper to buy than hardwoods.

When a tree is cut down, the logs are sawn into planks. The planks are left to dry in a process called seasoning. If this is not done carefully, the wood will twist or warp. A special kiln is often used to speed up the drying process. The wood is then cut into smaller pieces, ready to be used in lots of different ways.

Wood drying out slowly in the open air

Improving the properties of wood

If you look carefully at wood, you can see a pattern of lines. These are the fibres of wood. The pattern is called the grain. It is more difficult to cut wood across the grain because the fibres have to be broken.

Wood can be strengthened by sticking thin sheets together, with the grain of each sheet placed in a different direction. This strong material is called plywood. It is often used in the building industry.

Blockboard is also a strong, stiff material. It is made up of boards of wood glued together. These are sandwiched between thin sheets of wood called veneer.

Chipboard is a cheap material made of wood chips and sawdust glued together. It is often covered in a veneer and used to make furniture.

Wood can be coated with paint, wax or plastic to protect it from the weather. Other substances such as creosote are used to prevent woodworm eating it. Wood can also be treated to make it fireproof.

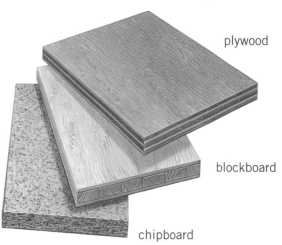

plywood

blockboard

chipboard

Wood can be turned into a range of useful materials.

Using wood

Wood is used to make all kinds of products. People have made homes from wood and used it as fuel for heating and cooking for thousands of years. Today the rainforests are being cut down for timber and to clear land for farming, but the trees are not being replaced. Unless the world does more to conserve its trees, we could start to run out of wood.

Wood is used to build homes in many countries because it is such a strong material. Even homes that are built of other materials still have wood in them. They often have timber frameworks, doors, floorboards and window frames.

Wood is also used to make furniture. It is easy to cut and join, and can be carved into all kinds of shapes. Wooden furniture can be coloured and polished to give an attractive appearance.

Many musical instruments are made from wood. Beautiful sounds are produced when the wood vibrates.

In the past, wood was an important material for building boats. Ships today are made of steel, but some sailing boats are still made of wood.

Houses often have timber frameworks.

walnut-veneer cabinet

beech chair

birch broom

oak barrel

willow basket

pine breadbin

sycamore violin

Wood is cut, carved, shaped and polished into all kinds of useful products.

Burning wood

Trees are cut down and used as the main fuel for heating and cooking in many parts of the world. Charcoal is a type of fuel made from wood. It is made by burning wood very slowly in kilns under large mounds of earth. Wood burns extremely well and causes little pollution, but growing enough trees to supply all needs is a problem.

In Britain, some farmers are using traditional methods of cutting wood without destroying the tree. Coppicing means cutting only part of the tree, leaving the rest to continue growing. This is an efficient way of using wood as a fuel.

Making charcoal in Brazil

Lots of useful chemicals are produced when wood is heated. Paint, varnish and disinfectants all use chemicals that come from wood. However, the most important chemical for life on Earth is oxygen.

Trees give out oxygen as they grow. When they burn, trees use up oxygen and produce carbon dioxide. The world has too much carbon dioxide already.

Fires smoulder as the rainforests are destroyed.

Conservation

Half the world's trees grow in the tropical rainforests around the equator. The rainforests are in great danger because so much wood is being taken from them, and it is not being replaced. If the rainforests are destroyed, the world will lose many types of animals and plants. It will also lose the vital source of oxygen which the trees provide.

Paper

Paper comes in all shapes, sizes and colours. Large amounts are used every day for writing and printing, boxes and packaging, tissues and much more.

Wasps make their nests from paper. They chew up wood to produce a pulp which hardens as it dries. The Chinese used this idea to make the first paper in AD 105. They mashed together tree bark and water, then poured the mixture onto bamboo matting to drain. Much later, the Chinese were the first people to use toilet paper and exam papers!

How paper is made

Paper is made from softwood trees grown specially for the paper industry. The trees are chopped down and taken to a factory called a paper-mill. The mill is sited near the forest where the trees are grown. Logs have the bark removed before being chopped into very small wood chips. The chips are ground up and mixed with water and chemicals to make a thick wet pulp.

The wood pulp is fed onto a conveyor belt, where the water drains away through a wire mesh. The web of paper gets drier and stronger as it runs through a series of rollers and heated cylinders. The dry paper is finally wound onto a huge roller, ready to be cut into sheets.

Wood chips at a paper-mill in Sweden

Water drains away as the wood pulp moves along the conveyor belt.

Huge rolls of finished paper

Different types of paper

Paper has lots of tiny fibres, which come from the wood. You can see the fibres in some papers better than others. Use a magnifying glass to look at the fibre structure in a soft type of paper such as kitchen roll.

Did you know?
The largest paper-making machines can produce a roll 25 metres wide at 1000 metres per minute. That is wider than a road, and faster than you can run!

The strength and absorbency of paper depends on the fibres. Tissues have an open fibre structure to absorb more liquid. Because cloth fibres are stronger than wood fibres, rags are added to wood pulp to make paper used for bank notes. Other properties can be given to paper by adding different substances at the paper-mill. Glue is added to make very strong paper, while a special type of glue makes paper waterproof. China clay, or kaolin, is used to coat the surface of writing paper to stop the ink from running. Cardboard is made of thick paper hardened with glue. It is made even stronger for packaging by giving it a corrugated shape.

Looking at tissue paper under a magnifying glass

New paper from waste

Paper products make up about one-third of people's rubbish. Most of this is packaging and newspapers. Waste paper can easily be recycled to make new paper. You can stop a tree being cut down each year by recycling your daily newspaper.

Recycling paper

Large quantities of waste paper are collected and taken to a paper-mill. Here the waste paper is shredded and the ink removed by chemicals. Sometimes the pulp is bleached to make the paper look whiter. The pulp is then added to wood pulp to make new paper.

Did you know?
A tree has to be cut down for every 400 copies of a newspaper.

Waste paper at a recycling plant

Make your own paper

1 Make a sieve and deckle

Make two identical wooden frames. Fix a fine material (e.g. old net curtain) to one to make the sieve. Fix four small pieces of hardboard to the other frame to make the deckle.

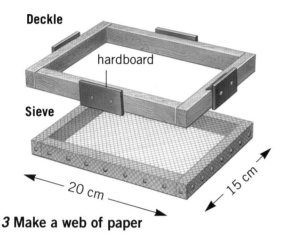

2 Pulp the paper

Leave small pieces of paper to soak overnight in warm water. Add washing-up liquid to help remove ink. Whisk or mash up the soft paper with a fork. Drain off excess water.

3 Make a web of paper

Put the deckle on top of the sieve and push into the paper mixture. Shake gently to get an even thickness. Remove carefully and leave to drain.

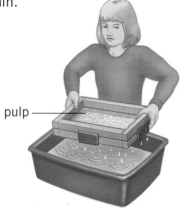

Special papers

You can add different ingredients to your pulp to make different types of paper. Add 2 teaspoons of starch to make writing paper. Use food colouring to colour the paper, or try blackberry or beetroot juice. Experiment with the leaves of plants such as mint or lavender to make scented paper.

4 Press the paper

Remove the deckle and lay the sieve pulp-side down on a board covered with kitchen roll. Rub the net to ease off the pulp and put a piece of kitchen roll on top. Make several sheets, then cover with a second board. Stand on top to squeeze out the water.

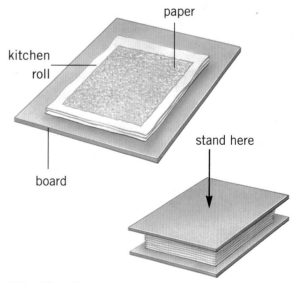

5 Dry the sheets

Separate the sheets and leave to dry. This will take about a day at room temperature.

Metals

Most metals have to be extracted from rocks in the Earth's crust. Metals are important in the history of humankind because of their many useful properties.

Did you know?
Aluminium makes up 8 per cent of the Earth's crust. Iron makes up 5 per cent.

Properties of metals

Metals are strong and hard. They are used to build machinery and structures for tall buildings. When heated, metals soften and then melt. They can be shaped when soft, or cast into new shapes when liquid.

Metals are shiny and silvery or golden in colour. Most react with the air to rust, corrode or tarnish. Only silver, gold and platinum keep their shine. All metals are good conductors of heat and electricity.

Red-hot liquid steel being cast at a foundry

Finding metals

Seventy of the 92 chemical elements are metals. Gold and silver are found as pure metals in the ground, but most metals combine with other chemical elements to form an ore. Separating the metal from the ore can be a difficult process. Ancient history is often divided into periods by the metals available at the time.

In the Stone Age, people had not discovered metals. They used rocks and animal and plant materials. About 5000 BC in Egypt and the Middle East, copper was extracted from the ore malachite. It was probably discovered by accident in a cooking fire. Copper ore was later heated with tin ore to produce bronze.

The Bronze Age lasted until 1500 BC, when iron was extracted from rock. The iron-making process requires a temperature hotter than a fire, so the Iron Age came about slowly as technology developed.

Sixteenth-century bronze sculpture from Nigeria

Nineteenth-century engraving showing Bessemer steel being made in Pittsburgh, USA

Although iron is strong, it is quite soft. The next important discovery was to add a small amount of charcoal (containing the element carbon) to turn it into steel. Because steel is a very hard metal, it was used to make swords and knives.

New processes for making iron brought about the Industrial Revolution of eighteenth-century Britain. Iron was used to build railways, bridges and factory machines. Machines and steam-power gave rise to great changes in people's lives.

In 1856, Henry Bessemer introduced a new method for making steel cheaply. Since that time, steel has been the world's most important construction material. More steel is used today than all other metals put together.

Making metals

The Earth is mined for rocks containing metal ores. The metal is extracted from its ore in many different ways. The process usually involves crushing and heating the ore to produce a chemical reaction.

Iron

Like most metals, iron is not found in the Earth as a pure metal. It combines with other chemical elements to form an ore. The iron is separated from its ore in a process called smelting.

Smelting

Iron ore is mixed with coke and limestone in a blast furnace. It is called a blast furnace because air is blasted through to produce a temperature of 1600 °C. The heat energy allows an important chemical reaction to take place between the carbon in the coke and the oxygen in the ore. It leaves behind the iron, mixed with a small amount of carbon. The molten (liquid) iron flows to the bottom of the furnace, where it is poured off. Impurities in the iron ore combine with the limestone to produce a waste material called slag.

loading iron ore,
coke and limestone

waste gase

hot air

molten iron

molte

m

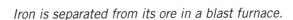

Iron is separated from its ore in a blast furnace.

Steel

The molten iron is still too impure to be very useful, so it is now refined to make steel. Oxygen is blasted into the molten metal to remove some of the carbon, while lime removes other impurities. Scrap steel is also added to recycle the metal.

The molten steel is poured out of the furnace and cast into bars, ready to be manufactured into different products. Most cars are made of steel. Steel plates are joined together by melting the edges. This is called welding.

Robots weld car bodies on a factory production line.

Copper and aluminium

Copper and aluminium are also important metals. Heat and electricity are needed to separate them from their ores.

Bars of aluminium at a factory in Dubai, United Arab Emirates

Copper is smelted from copper ore and then refined by an electrical process. Copper does not corrode and is an extremely good conductor of heat and electricity. Central heating pipes are made of copper, and electrical circuits are made of copper wire.

Aluminium is found in the mineral bauxite. It is a very reactive metal and has to be separated from its ore in an electrical process. Heat is created by passing electric currents through the bauxite. The rock melts and the aluminium floats to the surface.

Aluminium is one of the lightest metals and is used to make high-speed trains. It is also used for drinks cans and as wrapping on chocolate bars.

Using metals

Metals are an essential part of our world. We use them to make hundreds of different products and machines. Metals are expensive to produce and supplies will not last for ever. It is important that we recycle unwanted metal objects to save our world's resources.

Alloys

Pure metals are quite soft. Gold can be hammered into sheets which are so thin you can see through them. Metals need to be strengthened or hardened for many uses. This is done by adding another substance to the metal to make an alloy. For example, adding zinc to copper makes the alloy brass. Brass is a much stronger metal than pure copper.

Aluminium drinks cans ready to be recycled into aluminium sheets

bronze

stainless steel

brass

tungsten steel

Some common alloys

Brass is copper with zinc added. It is used for nuts and bolts because it is strong and does not corrode.

Bronze is copper with tin added. It is often used to make statues because the molten metal casts well.

Stainless steel is steel with chromium and nickel added. It is widely used for cutlery and surgical instruments because it does not rust.

Tungsten steel is steel with tungsten and chromium added. It is used to make cutting tools because it is a very hard metal.

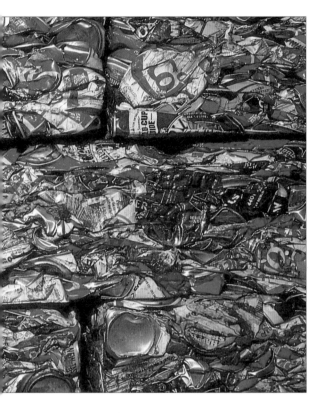

Corrosion

Corrosion is a chemical reaction between a metal and another chemical, usually oxygen in water or air. The reaction produces a new chemical substance. Iron, for example, forms rust. As well as looking unpleasant, rust and corrosion dangerously weaken metal structures. Metals can be painted or coated with plastics or other metals to protect them. Cars have seven protective layers painted on top of the metal surface. Steel dustbins are 'galvanised' with a coat of zinc.

Corrosion means that unwanted metals will disappear in time. Many metals are scarce, while others form poisonous solutions as they corrode. It is therefore important to recycle as much as possible. A good start can be made with the millions of aluminium drinks cans.

Sea water has corroded away the metal of Brighton's West Pier.

Fossil fuels

Coal, oil and natural gas are fossil fuels. They formed from the remains of plants, trees and tiny sea animals that lived on Earth millions of years ago. Fossil fuels are used to heat our homes and to transport us by road, rail and sea.

Coal

In prehistoric times, much of the land was covered by dense forest. As successive generations of trees and plants died, they became buried deeper and deeper in mud. The mud slowly turned into rock and pressed down on the layers of dead trees and plants, gradually turning them into a hard black material called coal. The chemicals from the prehistoric trees and plants that make coal burn well are called hydrocarbons.

Open-cast coal mining

Coal mining is a worldwide industry. Coal can sometimes be dug from close to the surface (open-cast mining), but it often has to be brought up from seams (layers) deep under the ground. Shafts are dug and the coal is cut from tunnels using powerful cutting machines.

Most of the world's coal is burned in power stations that generate electricity. Few homes now burn coal on household fires. Oil, gas and electricity are easier to use.

Coal is cut from deep seams hundreds of metres under the ground.

Oil and gas

Oil and gas are made from the remains of tiny sea animals. Their bodies sank to the sea bed millions of years ago and became buried under layers of sand and mud. Over many years, they turned into gas and oil.

Oil was discovered by accident in America in 1859. People soon realised how useful it was, and many became oil millionaires.

Today huge amounts of money are spent in the search for oil. Small boreholes are drilled deep into the Earth's surface. The oil is often found under the sea bed. Large offshore drilling platforms, like the one in the picture below, are built to withstand the roughest seas. Pipelines or oil tankers carry the oil to storage tanks on land.

North Sea oil platform off the coast of Scotland

Materials from oil

Oil is a remarkably useful material and has changed the world since it was discovered last century. Petrol and plastics are made from oil, and so are many medicines, cosmetics and paints.

An oil refinery

Oil is found as crude oil (petroleum). Before it can be used, crude oil has to be refined in large factories called refineries. The oil is heated in a tower, and then carefully cooled to separate all the different parts. Gasoline (petrol) is the most useful part. It is also the lightest part and condenses at the top of the tower. The heavier parts condense at the bottom.

Oil is a source of many useful chemicals. It is used to make detergents, fertilisers, paints, dyes, drugs, fibres and plastics.

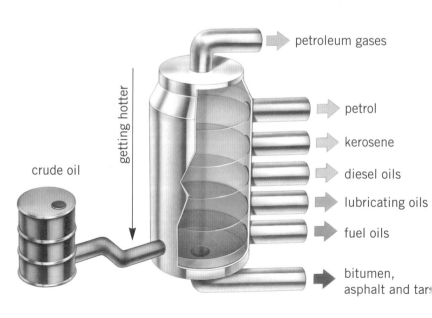

getting hotter

crude oil

petroleum gases

petrol

kerosene

diesel oils

lubricating oils

fuel oils

bitumen, asphalt and tar

Oil is separated into different parts at the refinery.

petrol

bitumen for road tarmac

plastics for CDs
and tapes

butane gas for
heat and light

paints

Products made from oil

Global warming

Most of the world's road, air and sea transport runs on oil. Light oils such as petrol are easy to transport. They burn to give lots of energy but no smoke or ash. So much oil is needed that supplies may run out in the near future.

Burning oil and gas produces water and carbon dioxide. The increase in the amount of carbon dioxide produced each year is affecting the Earth's climate. Carbon dioxide traps the heat of the sun, like the glass of a greenhouse, and causes global warming. Exhaust fumes from cars contain carbon dioxide (produces global warming), soot (produces smog) and lead (a poison). We need to cut down our use of fossil fuels to avoid pollution and to conserve supplies for the future.

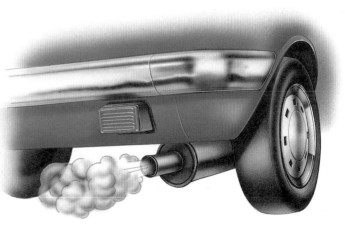

Rubber

Rubber bands are made to stretch and rubber balls bounce. They show the same important property of rubber: it is elastic. This means it will return to its normal shape after being stretched or squashed.

Rubber is also tough, waterproof, and can easily be moulded into special shapes when liquid. These properties make it an extremely useful material.

Collecting latex from cuts made in the bark of a rubber tree in Ghana

Natural rubber

Have you ever noticed the sticky white liquid that comes out the broken stem of plants such as dandelions? It is called latex. When latex dries, it forms a rubbery seal to protect the plant against germs and insects. Rubber trees, grown mainly in Malaysia, produce lots of latex. Cuts are made in the bark and the latex is collected in cups. It is then shipped all over the world.

Did you know?
The glue Copydex is almost pure latex. If you mix it with a little vinegar, you can turn it into rubber.

Manufacturing rubber

Pure natural rubber is soft and sticky. In 1839, Charles Goodyear discovered that heating latex with sulphur made a stronger, more elastic material. This process is called vulcanisation. He used the new rubber to make car tyres.

Nowadays the latex is mixed and heated with other substances to give rubber lots of different properties. Elastic and waterproof properties make it very useful for sports equipment and for gloves for washing up.

1950s advertisement for Goodyear tyres

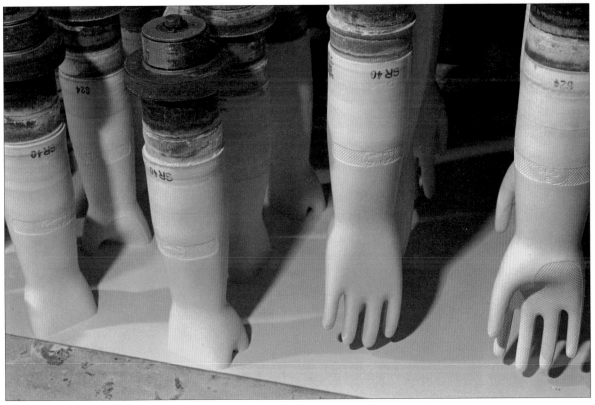

Glove formers are dipped in latex to make rubber gloves.

Plastics

Plastics have been designed to take the place of other materials, such as metals and wood. There are many different kinds of plastics, but they all have certain properties in common.

All plastics are good insulators of heat and electricity. They can be made strong or flexible, heavy or light, transparent or any colour you like. They last a very long time because they do not rot or corrode. In fact it is difficult to get rid of most plastics.

Making plastics

The first plastics were made of cellulose. This is a natural substance that gives strength and flexibility to the stems and leaves of plants. Viscose was invented in 1912. It is made by dissolving wood pulp (contains cellulose) in caustic soda. The syrupy viscose liquid is squirted into fibres and used to make clothing, carpets, tea-bags and disposable nappies. The viscose syrup can also be squeezed into a thin film and used to make adhesive tape and wrappings for sweets and crisps.

In the 1930s, scientists discovered how to make the long chain-shaped molecules found in cellulose. The chemical process is called polymerisation, which explains why there are a lot of 'poly-' plastics. Some very important new plastics were invented at this time, including polythene, nylon and perspex. Most plastics are made from chemicals which come from oil.

Viscose fibres being spun into threads

Thermosets and thermoplastics

There are two main groups of plastics: thermosets and thermoplastics. They behave in different ways. Thermosets do not soften when heated but will burn if heated to a very high temperature. Thermosets are used for pan handles, kitchen tops and to cover plugs and wires which carry electricity.

Thermoplastics melt and change shape when heated. Polythene, nylon, PVC and polystyrene are all thermoplastics.

Polythene

covering for electical wires

bucket

toy duck

Nylon

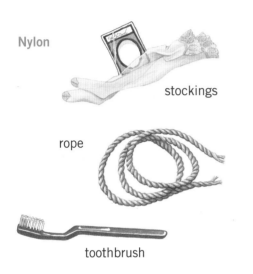

stockings

rope

toothbrush

Polystyrene

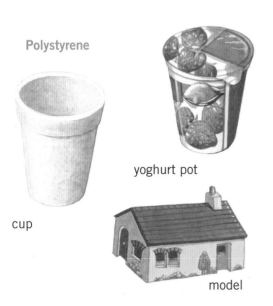

yoghurt pot

cup

model

PVC

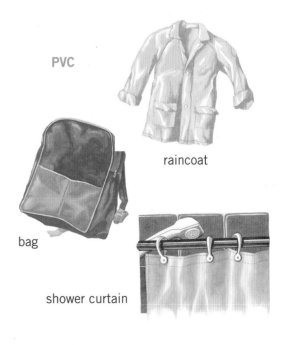

raincoat

bag

shower curtain

Products made from thermoplastics

Fabrics

Natural or synthetic fibres are joined together to make flexible, hard-wearing fabrics. When fabrics are used for clothing, they are called cloth, textiles or just 'material'.

Making fabrics

Felt garments were first made in Turkey over 7500 years ago. Felt is made by simply pressing together and heating fibres. Nowadays, fibres are usually rolled together to produce threads in a process called spinning.

Threads are woven on a loom to make fabric. Weaving uses two threads, the warp and the weft. The warp is fixed to the frame, while the weft weaves its way under and over. The clothing industry uses huge fast-moving machines to weave fabric.

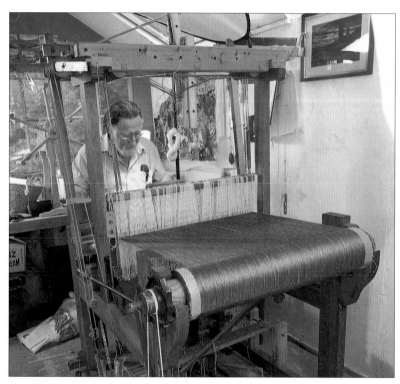

Hand-operated weaving loom

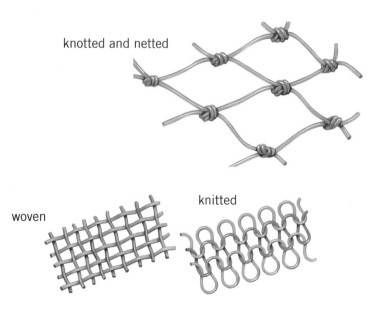

knotted and netted

woven

knitted

Different ways of fixing threads together

You may have tried other ways of making fabrics by hand. A single thread, for example, can be knitted or knotted and netted. The gap between the threads allows air to pass through the fabric. This makes clothes comfortable to wear. In woven fabrics, the gap is so small that you may need a magnifying glass to see it. In knitted fabrics, such as jumpers, the gap is much larger and helps to insulate the wearer from the cold.

Synthetic fabrics

Scientists have found ways of making a wide variety of synthetic fibres and fabrics. Although synthetic fabrics behave in a similar way to natural fabrics, they are often stronger and cheaper to buy. Many are made from oil. One of the first fabrics to be made from oil was nylon. Invented in the 1930s by American scientist William Carothers as a cheap alternative to silk, nylon is strong, flexible and light. It quickly found important uses as women's stockings, which were called 'nylons', and as parachute fabric during World War II.

Fabrics for special uses

Fabrics can be made to have special properties. Some fabrics used in the home must be able to resist fire. They can be treated with chemicals to make them fire-resistant, or even better is to choose a fabric that is not affected by heat. Fire blankets are made from glass fibre because it does not burn.

A 1940s film star tries on the first pair of nylons to come off the looms following the war.

Fabrics can be waterproof, strong, hard-wearing, colourful, smooth or rough. Clothes designers think how a fabric is to be used when choosing the right material for a garment. What properties do you think a mountaineer's clothes and equipment must have? Turn to page 48 to check your answer.

Sportswear and equipment made from synthetic fibres

Materials for the future

Materials are being researched and developed by material scientists all the time. Here are just a few examples of some exciting new materials and their special properties.

Chris Boardman wins a gold medal at the 1992 Olympics

Olympic cyclist Chris Boardman won a gold medal at the 1992 Olympics in Barcelona. A new material manufactured from carbon fibres was used to build the frame of his bike. It made the bike very strong and lightweight.

Some materials are designed to replace parts of the body. Dentists have used metal fillings for a long time. Although strong, they do not look like teeth. New plastic materials look more natural and stick to the tooth much better than metal.

Window glass can be manufactured so that it goes dark in sunlight. This makes buildings more comfortable to work in and saves energy.

Materials developed for one purpose can sometimes be useful for other things too. Teflon is a strong plastic that was developed to seal the fuel tanks in space rockets. It is now used to coat cooking pans because it stops food sticking to the metal.

Completely new materials such as 'buckyball' are sometimes discovered. Buckyball is a type of carbon with football-shaped molecules. Its full name is buckminsterfullerene, after the person who designed a building in Montreal which had this structure. Material scientists of the future will find out how this new material can be used!

Buckyball molecules are shaped like the building below.

This twenty-storey dome in Montreal was built for an exhibition in 1967.

Index

Published by BBC Educational Publishing, a division of BBC Education, BBC White City, 201 Wood Lane, London W12 7TS
First published 1994
© Martin Hollins/BBC Education
The moral right of the author has been asserted.

Paperback ISBN: 0 563 39655 5
Hardback ISBN: 0 563 39782 9

Colour reproduction by Radstock Reproductions Ltd
Cover origination in England by Radstock Reproductions Ltd
Printed and bound by BPC Paulton Books Ltd

Illustrations: © Julian Baker 1994 (pages 8, 13, 22, 23, 27, 29, 32, 38, 39, 44 and 47), © Jan Hill 1994 (pages 16, 24, 34, 39 and 43), © John Shipperbottom 1994 (pages (pages 2–3 and 9)

Photo credits: The Advertising Archives **p. 41 (top)**; Allsport **p. 46**; British Coal **p. 36 (bottom)**; BBC/Luke Finn **pp. 4, 7, 21 (top)**; British Library **p. 31 (left)**; Crafts Council/Peter Chatterton **p. 17 (bottom)** *glaze fired* earthenware pot by Kate Malone; Crown Copyright **p. 11 (bottom)**; Ecoscene **pp. 15 (right), 26 (bottom), 27**; Environmental Picture Library **p. 25**; Evening Argus/Simon Dack **p. 35**; Paul Felix **p. 44**; Barry Finch Photography **p. 42**; Geoscience Features Picture Library **pp. 8 (left), 11 (bottom)**; Robert Harding Picture Library **pp. 12 (left); 15 (left), 17 (top), 20 (top), 23, 24, 26 (top), 28, 30, 33 (left), 37, 38, 40, 45 (bottom), 47**; Michael Holford **pp. 12 (right), 31 (right)**; Hulton Deutsch Collection **p. 45 (top)**; ICCE/Mark Boulton **pp. 34/35**; LRC Products Ltd **p. 41 (bottom)**; Photo courtesy of MIRA - Motor Industry Research Association **p. 5**; The Natural History Museum **pp. 8 (right), 10, 11 (top)**; NHPA/Stephen Dalton **p. 20 (bottom)**; Pilkington Glass Ltd **p. 19**; Science Photo Library **pp. 14, 18 (bottom), 22, 36 (top)**, Still Pictures **pp. 6, 18 (top), 21 (bottom)**; Tony Stone Images **p. 33 (right)**; Weald and Downland Open Air Museum/Bob Powell **p. 13**

Front cover: The Natural History Museum **(main picture)** *iron pyrite*; BBC/Luke Finn **(bottom right)** *glass marbles*

Answers to page 45: *jacket* (synthetic fabric) strong, waterproof, flexible; *rucksack* (nylon) strong, waterproof coating; *trousers* (polyester cotton) comfortable, warm; *boots* (nylon and leather) comfortable, tough, waterproof, soles able to grip; *rope* (nylon) strong and weather-resistant